D1541928

1 the 2004 State Championship, my son Ben tore the patella tendon
f his bone. He missed all the next season, but thanks to Jeremy, Ben
is able to play football again in 2006. Jeremy helped my son
come physically fit, emotionally strong, and go on to play football in
llege. It's not how you start, its how you finish when it comes to
hletic performance. And just like athletes, Jeremy's book **Parent**
ur Best will make sure every Sports Parent finishes strong. "

1 Jorden- Executive Producer NFL & NASCAR

he unconditional love, nurturing, and support of a sporting parent
e the important contributing factors in the development of young
hletes in all sports. Jeremy's book will help you be the best Sporting
rent for your child you can be."

ayne Goldsmith- World renowned Sports Performance Expert and
ner of www.sportscoachingbrain.com

eremy has the unique ability to help parents and athletes establish
eir definition of 'family excellence' and provide the tools to build
d maintain healthy relationships that remain strong even during
aracter building times."

th Ebert- Charlotte, NC

Parent Your Best

Be the Reason Your Child Succeeds In Sport

Jeremy Boone

ISBN-13:
978-0615471884 (Athlete By Design Press)
ISBN-10:
0615471889

Published by:

This book is available in higher quantities and group/team discounts. For more information please visit www.parentyourbest.com.

Additional Resources and Seminars by Jeremy Boone

Coach Your Best
Ready To Play
Get Faster Now
Lower Body Performance for Sport
(ACL Prevention)

You can find Jeremy online at the following websites

www.parentyourbest.com
www.athletebydesign.com
www.sportsaxiology.com
www.coachyourbest.com

The book is dedicated to my two sons Will and Jay.
Thank you for teaching me something new each day and I hope
at I can be the dad that you both need me to be for years to come.

Acknowledgments

ost of the information in this book comes from what I have learned
om some key individuals throughout my coaching years as well as
y own unique experiences in life and in sport. There are many
ople that need to be acknowledged for Parent Your Best™ as no
ok is written by one person alone. However, there are a few key
lividuals that have played the biggest role in helping this vision
come a reality.

st and foremost I want to thank my own parents for all that they
ve taught me, how to handle both the good and the bad in life.
d while my mom passed away from cancer when I was younger, I
ow that she is smiling right now as she has been such a huge
spiration for me. And to my father, for continuing to teach me life's
sson of never giving up, no matter what life takes away from you.

ank you Dr. Dave and Vera Mefford for all that you continue to
ach me about the wonderful world of *Formal Axiology*. It is
cause of our friendship that I was able to connect my passion and
rpose in what I hope to bring to the world of sport with you both. I
nsider you both part of my family!

ould like to thank Jim Jordan for all of the effort he has put in to
ooting video and helping to spread this vision. I am most grateful
r our amazing friendship and thankful for all that you continue to
ach me about being a great Sport's Dad.

big thank you goes out to Amy Jamerson. If it were not for you, this
ok would not have been able to fulfill its intention. I am forever
ateful for all of the countless hours of helping me read, write, and
it, but even more so for our numerous conversations about what
e is really all about.

lso want to thank Tom Jamerson, Amy's husband, for being a
unding board and testing ground in helping to bring clarity in these
inciples and exercises. His vision for adding value to the lives of

athletes, coaches, and parents is truly second to none. Most importantly thank you for being such a great friend.

I am thankful for all of the families who have allowed me to work with them over the years and develop friendships that go well beyond a workout. Although too numerous to list, you know who you are.

I want to thank my close friends Beau Snyder, Mike Zagora, and Meg Locke for all of your support and encouragement through this process.

Last but not least, I want to thank God for all of the many undeserved blessings that he continues to give to me each day. I can't wait to see how this journey continues to unfold!

Table of Contents

Foreword

Wayne Goldsmith

"Every parent in the world, at some time, will become a Sporting Parent."

orting Parents (i.e. a sporting parent can mean a biological parent, reer, family support network – whoever is directly responsible for e care and upbringing of a child), can be and in most cases are, the y element in the sporting success of a young athlete.

- Coaches are important.
- Talent can be a vital ingredient.
- The skills and techniques of the sport - essential.
- A strong desire to succeed – fundamental.
- The belief that anything is possible – crucial.

t without the unconditional love and support of a parent, regiver, or significant nurturing adult, the chances of sporting ccess are limited.

ill comes down to potential.

hat every parent wants more than anything is to see their child alize their potential by taking full advantage of every opportunity esented to them: in school, in society, in their family life and in orts.

A coach can teach children to realize their potential as players, as athletes, and as performers.

A child can help themselves to realize their full potential by giving their heart, mind, and spirit to their training and preparation.

And a parent can help children realize their potential by teaching all the things that only parents can teach:

- Values – e.g. honesty, integrity, humility, courage, discipline
- Virtues – e.g. respect, enthusiasm, reliability, responsibility, loyalty, determination
- Manners
- Self-confidence / self-belief

Parents are partners in potential.

Just as there is no complete manual on how to be a good parent, being a good sporting parent requires a bit of training, effort, and education.

Parents love their children and want nothing but the best for them. What others may see as "pushy", sporting parents see as "lovingly supportive". While a coach may interpret a "sticking their nose in" type of parental behavior, sporting parents see only as a genuine interest in their child's development.

This difference in perspective and the difficulty in being objective where their kids are concerned often lead parents to a conflict situation with coaches, other parents, officials, and eventually their own children.

Many times parents have said *"I hear what you say, but you don't know my child. She is different".* While every child is indeed a unique

dividual, what child athletes have in common are parents with high
inions of their child's ability to do everything.

starts early – the first day home from the hospital.

*ere is a picture of my baby. He is the most beautiful baby I have
er seen and I am not just saying that because he is mine"*

ound two years of age:

*ly child is much more advanced than the other children – talking
d walking before other kids, and I am not just saying that because
is mine".*

en at school.

*e is well advanced for his age. He can do things that most five year
ds can't. I'm not just saying that because he is my son".*

en naturally at sport.

*e is the best full back (or swimmer or runner or batter or goal
orer) in the district. He really is. I'm not just saying that because he
my son".*

any sporting parents believe that their child has talent in their
osen sport.

ow much talent the child actually has can be a result of many
ctors: genetics, training, diet, how old they were when they took up
e sport, flexibility, growth and maturation.

s, however, a fact that sporting parents must accept from their first
volvement in sport that:

- Not All Kids Are Champions;
- Kids Can Not Win Everything They Contest;
- They Cannot Always Be The Best — Nor Should You Expect Them To Be;
- Not All Kids Are Great In The First Sport They Try;
- Not All Kids Will Always Be Great At The Same Sport They First Succeed In;
- Not All Kids Will Be Great In The Same Event Or Same Position In The Same Sport;
- Not All Kids Will Be Good At Any Sport.

It's all about potential.

It would be great to see every child who takes up any sport become a world record holder or a professional athlete or an Olympic champion. That would be fantastic.

But, do you know what would be even better?

To know that every child who takes up any sport realizes their full potential as a person and as a result of their sports experience lives a long, happy, healthy life being all they can be.

Talent is not as important as tenacity and team spirit.

Running is not as important as resilience and respect.

Power is not as important as passion and perseverance.

Height is not as important as humility and hard work.

Agility is not as important as attitude and the ability to overcome adversity.

tential comes from developing the person first....then the person n become anything they choose to be....a teacher, a successful siness person, a writer, a builder, a professional athlete, an ympic champion and eventually a sporting parent themselves.

d the group of people who are best placed, best capable, best otivated, and best able to develop quality human beings are rents.

, enjoy being a sporting parent.

ing part of something which can help your child realize their tential not just as players and athletes but as human beings can be vonderful and rewarding experience.

d most importantly, play your part.

u expect the coach to be the best he / she can be.

u expect your child to be the best he / she can be.

ially, expect yourself to be the best sporting parent you can be. emy's book is a great start.

an integral part: a partner in potential with your child and their ach and there are no limits to what the three of you can achieve gether.

G

vw.sportscoachingbrain.com

Introduction

Jeremy Boone

'A child is not a person to be molded, but a person to be unfolded."
-Author unknown

ιe **of my favorite American sitcoms is the Bernie Mac Show.** It is
out the comedian Bernie Mac raising his sister's three children and
/es his unique perspective on being a parent. In the season three
isode titled 'The Eye of the Tiger' Jordan, the frail middle nephew,
cides to try out for the basketball team in order to please his Uncle
rnie. As you can imagine, Bernie is so excited that he brings out his
ἱ high school jersey to give to Jordan and starts to relive his glory
ys. However, due to Jordan's complete lack of athleticism he ends
joining the gymnastics team. Now at first Bernie Mac was
palled at the idea, but then Jordan convinces him that he is going
attempt the rings, a man's event.

ι the day of Jordan's first gymnastics meet, Bernie Mac is so excited
brings one of his friends to help cheer Jordan on. Then the
ɔment of truth happens, the announcer calls out Jordan's name and
;tead of competing in the rings, he runs out onto the gym floor
ιving a giant ribbon on a stick! Bernie Mac is completely stunned!
ith his own pride and self-image now damaged, he turns and tells
; friend that no one else can know about what just happened.

By the end of the episode, Bernie successfully gets Jordan to quit the gymnastics team. Eventually he realizes that Jordan does enjoy it, and Bernie has to put aside his own self-pride to be the parent that Jordan needs him to be. The episode ends with Jordan rejoining the team; back out on the gym floor waving his ribbon wand, and Bernie Mac confidently cheering him on.

So what about you? When it comes to your child participating in sports, how many Bernie Mac moments have you struggled with?

"How did the whole Parent Your Best™ vision get started?"

Like all inspiring visions that often start with a burden, Parent Your Best™ has stemmed from my work with training thousands of student athletes since 1996. What was most frustrating for me was to see these young men and women work so hard to change their bodies and acquire new skills, but then are unable to effectively translate these new gains to the field, court, or ice. Searching for the reasons why, I finally realized that the problem was not solely with the athletes themselves, it was also due to an unhealthy relationship with their parents.

On one occasion, I ran into a former athlete a few years after she graduated high school asking her how she was doing and what her parents were up to. I then asked her about playing soccer and with a look of disgust on her face she replied *"We don't talk about sports at all in my family after what happened with my parents. What should be remembered as a fun experience in high school is instead a freaking nightmare."*

In 2007 I was introduced to Dr. Dave and Vera Mefford, who I now consider extended family, and with them became involved in developing a new mental performance profile for athletes based on Sports Axiology (the science of human value and decision making in sport). Since then, I have reviewed just over two thousand mental profiles of high school athletes looking at their mental strengths and weaknesses. The results showed that many of these athletes were feeling a lot of stress and tension from outside themselves which was ecting other mental attributes such as self-confidence, mental ughness, self-esteem, self-worth, and self-motivation.

just what was this 'outside' source? You guessed it...for many of em it was pressure from their parents! A small percentage was due overbearing parents, but many of the cases involved normal hard orking parents and basically healthy families. It was the athletes emselves who felt they needed to reach the next level in order to t disappoint their mom or dad.

is research provided tangible proof beyond my own coaching periences of the negative impact that an unhealthy parent-child ationship can have on and off the field. As a result, I set out on a urney that would hopefully allow me to impact an entire culture in ositive way... the culture of Sports Parents.

egan by asking myself a few questions:

- What was great about my relationship with my parents as a young athlete?
- How could our relationship have been even better in relation to my youth sports experience?
- If I had known then what I know now, how would that have impacted my relationship with my parents as well as my performance?
- Of all of the athletes I have worked with, what were the qualities and attributes of the sports parents who seemed to 'get it'?
- What were the qualities and attributes of the sports parents that often led to family feuds and even their child's athletic burnout?
- What about those parents who honestly had no idea of the unintentional stress they were putting on their child to perform?
- What would be some KEY sports parenting principles, tools, and skills that parents of today's young athletes need to know in order to have a healthy family relationship that at the end

of the day positively affects the young athletes' performance and their enjoyment of the game?

- What media format and platform should be used to educate sports parents in a non-judgmental way?

The answers to these questions and many more are found in this book.

What this book will not tell you

Parent Your Best™ is by no means meant to be the definitive answer to sports parenting. Although the concepts, principles, and exercises in this book are helpful for any parent, it is not meant for the Sports Parents you see on the news assaulting coaches or other parents. This type of parent only makes up 10% or less of the total Sports Parent culture.

You will not find specific answers to the top twenty problems that sports parents face on a daily basis. Actually, there is already a good resource for this type of quick solution book which I will tell you about later in the book. One final but very important point, it is not meant to serve as counseling or therapy for struggling families, as I am not a counselor, but rather a coach.

So who exactly is this book for?

It is written for the other 90% of Sports Parents just like you who have high aspirations for their children in sport, who find themselves trying to survive week to week with their family life dictated by their children's sports, and for some, who are simply tired of a stressful marriage completely built around youth sports.

Just like your child has a coach to help them learn sports skills, design practices and routines to develop those skills, and then through games display those skills, EVERY SPORTS PARENT NEEDS A COACH, including you!

low are a few of the key skills that are critical to being a Sports
rent:

Listening	Patience
Communication	Praise
Connection	Recognition
Empowerment	Engagement
Leadership	Empathy
Decision Making	Respect
Support	Time Management

ave been extremely blessed to have met and built meaningful
ationships with many families over the years, some of whom you
ll meet in this book, and who in many ways are probably similar to
ur own family.

e principles and exercises in this book are a result of those
ationships, including a blueprint to help you build the skills and
ols you need to be the best sports parent for your child.

ou let it, the information you are about to discover will be a life
anger for you as a Sports Parent.

m enthusiastic and honored to be a part of your team!

How to get the most out of this book

is book is designed to be a self-coaching guide for Sports Parents
d is not meant for you to read from cover to cover in a single sitting
though please feel free to do so). To get the most out of this book,
uggest doing the following:

1. Read the introduction so that you will get a clear understanding of the purpose of this book, why I wrote it.

2. Ideally, you will get the most out of this book if you read each chapter in sequential order so you can build on what you learn from each previous chapter. At the end of each chapter you will find the Parent Your Best™ Workout filled with various exercises and activities to help you build a particular Sports Parenting skill. Some exercises will be just for you and/or your spouse, while others will involve your entire family. There is also a link provided to access an online resource filled with various worksheets and other special bonuses.

3. After you have completed all of the exercises and worked through them with your family at the end of each chapter, proceed to the next chapter and repeat step three. Follow these steps until you have completed chapters 1-5 in the book.

4. If you have more than one child, be sure to work through each of the questions and exercises separately. Every child is different!

5. Once you have completed the entire book, go back and use it as a resource for each new sports season. It will serve as an excellent bumper rail for both you and your family as to what matters most.

6. I would love to hear any of your stories or experiences from the book! Let me know by visiting www.twitter.com/parentyourbest or comment on www.facebook.com/parentyourbest

When it comes to building a House of Champions, it's like my friend and former Pro-Bowl NFL Wide Receiver Muhsin Muhammad always says… *"You can't rush greatness!"*

Ch.1 Parent Your Best™- The Mindset

*"My dad always said that how you respond
to adversity is everything."*- Ben Jorden

) you ever feel like at times you are on a roller coaster ride that
·ver stops when it comes to your child participating in youth sports?
ιve you ever reached your tipping point during a conversation with
ur child on the way home after a game and were ready to throw in
ε towel? If there is one thing I can promise you it's that I definitely
derstand what you are going through! How do I know this? By not
ving any idea of what I was getting into back in 1996.

rst started my own sports performance training business in
ιarlotte, NC, with the sole purpose of helping young athletes
prove their speed and strength. Marketing my services was
tually pretty easy back then because performance training had just
ιrted to become popular and there were very few individuals who
'ered this service. All I had to do was to ask parents if their child
ιs struggling with speed, strength, or agility in their sport to strike
 a conversation. In fact, to this day I don't think a parent has ever
ιd no.

y dream, or so I thought at the time, would be to train student
ιletes every day after school, and then get to watch them play on
ε weekends. What a life, right? Wow, was I wrong. Little did I
˙ow that I would be spending just as much time, if not more, with
ε athletes' parents!

15

I was either going to be one of the reasons that their child experienced athletic success, or the sole reason that their child never made it. I also took on many other unexpected roles such as learning how to become a third party mediator between parents and their kids, a world class magician when parents had to have their son faster by the weekend for the upcoming 'elite' tournament, and a grief counselor for moms when things were not going right for little Johnny who totally deserved to be the winner because he tried hard.

I have had countless conversations with Sports Parents just like you about everything from coaches who show unfair favoritism to the stresses of upcoming team tryouts. All of this is to say that to be a parent in general we all must be a little crazy - and highly versatile, but to be a Sports Parent you've got to be super human!

Think of the mile long list of things that you have to deal with as a Sports Parent; annual dues, travel schedules, equipment costs, clothing expenses (hey, they gotta look good!), extra coaching sessions, the hike in your monthly food bill, etc. And those are just for starters!

Better yet, how about all of the stress that you have to deal with during their season: will they play well, is he going to start, I hope she doesn't get hurt, the coach better not bench him, we have to get a win today, she needs more exposure for college, will he make it through tryouts, and the list goes on.

Writing this makes me think about stories such as Jim Jorden, a good friend and father who struggled to enjoy watching his son play football because he could not control the outcome. On game days he was always more stressed out than his son and at times, because of the stress, he would find himself in a bad mood. His breakthrough occurred when he realized that it wasn't his game to play and he didn't make the calls. A few years ago, his son was hurt playing football in high school and almost lost the chance to play his senior year because of a faulty knee surgery and the school said he would not be allowed to play. What could have been a career ending

oment, turned into a father fighting for his son's right to play a
ort that his son loved. His son has now gone on to win a Division I-
\ national football college championship and four conference titles.

lso think about the father who was recently banned from watching
; daughter's club soccer games for the rest of the year.   During the
;h school soccer season, he was the calm parent. But when club
ason started, it was like Dr. Jekyll & Mr. Hyde. A parent from the
her team was complaining to the ref about his daughter and called
r a derogatory name. Out of love for his daughter, the attack and
otect button went off in his head and on instinct he jumped up and
ysically beat the other dad. Yes, he was embarrassed after the fact
d certainly regretted his actions. Does it make him a horrible
her? No, but he did make a poor decision letting his emotions and
ide get the best of him, which ended up negatively impacting not
ly his family but his daughter's entire team. He could have easily
iced blame on the other dad for his actions, but in the end he took
sponsibility for his own choices, focused on improving himself, and
eir family has become stronger for it.

ese stories and many more that I will share with you are about
orts Parents, good hearted people who just like you, would do
ything for their son or daughter. Yes, they struggled like we all do,
t in the end, these parents focused on what matters most, their
lationship with their child.

ie Global Impact of Parents in Youth Sports

ifortunately, youth sports have now turned into professional youth
orts. Competition is greater than ever before and the pressure to
 number one has never been higher. For example, athletes are
ecializing at much younger ages, children are sticking to a single
ar round sport, and burnout by the age of thirteen in the US is at an
-time high.

fact, this intense competitive mindset and pressure to be number
e in youth sports is felt around the world. A poll conducted by the

marketing research firm Ipsos found that four out of every ten adults (40%) had witnessed other adults being physically or verbally abusive to coaches and officials at a youth sporting event.

However, when looking at the data of 23,000 adults in twenty-two countries, it is the US that leads the crazy Sports Parent race with 60% of adults having seen another parent raging out of control.

And do you want to know the irony in all of this? According to a landmark study performed by Michigan State's Institute for the Study of Youth Sports, the number one reason that kids play sports is to have fun. Winning did not even make the top ten list!

Are you highly competitive?

Let me ask you this, what does competition and this craving to be number one look like in your own family? Do the experiences from being a part of your child's sport consistently bring out the best in you?

Bringing competition into your family's sport culture can be a good thing. The problem comes when your own competitive mindset and desires for your child take over. Do you focus more on preparing the path for your child rather than preparing your child to handle their own path?

So what's at stake if your competitive mindset dominates in your family?

It can teach your child that others (peers, coaches, teammates, and family members) are more of an obstacle to their own success and achievement, making it difficult to view them as friends and develop healthy collaborative relationships. It can also create an environment where your child doesn't know how to deal with failure, especially if your focus is more on a reward, winning, or any other outcome-based expectation.

ally, having a highly competitive mindset as a Sport Parent can lead
a performance-based relationship with your child. In other words,
becomes difficult for your child to separate how they perform from
o they are as a person.

t guess what? Making one simple mindset change can mean the
ference between survival and significance in parenting your best.

1e Sports Parent Dichotomy

e purpose of playing a sport is to win the game, to be the best. You
int your child to have the best coach, you want them to be the best
what they do, and you want to be the best parent you can be or
;e you would not be reading this book.   But what does it really
2an to be the best when it comes to being a Sports Parent?

st, let me tell you the three biggest lies when it comes to being the
st Sports Parent:

1. The best Sports Parent means you must buy your child the
    most expensive training equipment and brand name clothing
    such as Nike, Addidas, or Under Armour. How can your child
    be the best if they don't look like the best?

2. The best Sports Parent means you must spend all of your free
    time with them, for example attending every practice,
    traveling to every road game, or sacrificing your own mental
    and physical health

3. The best Sports Parent means all of your child's teammates
    and their parents treat you like an icon, that you in some way
    added value to the history of your child's game.

) any of these resonate with you? If so, here are a few thoughts on
ly being the best:

- **Best doesn't always mean perfect.** Too often parents associate these two words as the same when they are not. In fact, there is no such thing as the Perfect Parent!

- **Best doesn't always mean first place.** Sometimes our best isn't enough to be a championship parent on a daily basis. But the best that you are able to be on any given day is all your child needs and desires.

- **Best doesn't mean it's all about you.** Parenting your best is actually the opposite. If it's all about you then you're not being parent.

- **Best doesn't mean all eyes are on you.** When you are at your best as a parent, it's normal to want some of the focus and attention on you, you deserve it. In fact, you should get the MVP award (*short for Most Valuable Parent*). However, this award isn't given based on a single event or act. It's like being an NFL Offensive Lineman, they do all of the dirty work protecting the quarterback and setting him up so he can make the play, yet they don't get any of the glory. But in the end when you win the Super Bowl, everyone celebrates and you finally get acknowledged.

The Parent Your Best™ Mindset

When it comes to being your best as a parent, I want to challenge you with the following:

Instead of making your goal trying to be the best Sports Parent IN the world, turn it around and be the best Sports Parent FOR the world.

This shifts the focus away from you and puts it on your child.

By the word 'world' I really mean wherever you are at any given time and whoever you are with. For example, if you are attending your

ild's game, then the goal is to be the best Sports Parent FOR your
ild as their number one fan. If you are out in the back yard with
ur child practicing soccer or baseball, the goal is to be the best
orts Parent FOR your child as their supportive partner in developing
eir potential.

other great benefit from adopting this new mindset is that it
mpletely expands your own definition of the best version of you as
Sports Parent. So much so, that the best version of you will be a
essing, not a burden, for your child in sport and in life.

 *I would love to hear how you define what it
means to parent your best! Let me know on the
Facebook page Parent Your Best™.*

he Parent Your Best™ Mindset Workout

ay here is what I want you to do. Get out a sheet of paper and
ork through the following questions. Or you can go online to
ww.parentyourbest.com/bookresources and download the
orksheet for helping you develop the Parent Your Best Mindset.

Questions

- What does being competitive look like in their sport?

- How would being the best FOR the world change your perspective as a parent?

- How would your child benefit from your adopting this mindset?

- How would it impact your child if they had COMPLETE CONFIDENCE that you cared more about them being the best FOR the world as opposed to the best IN the world?

- What would happen if your child adopted the *Be the Best FOR the World*™ mindset?

Exercise

- Sit down with your child and discuss the definition of healthy versus unhealthy competition.

In the next chapter I am going to share with you the game plan for parenting your best. And like any game plan, it will only be as good as your ability to execute it!

Ch.2 Parent Your Best™- The Game Plan

"Parenting your best is about leveraging your game plan, not relying on one."

here did you learn to be a parent? Unfortunately, there isn't a
w-to manual given to new parents entitled 'The Blueprint for
ising a Brilliant, Healthy, Always Happy and Obedient Child with
orld Class Athletic Potential- 100% Guaranteed'. Instead, we
arned parenting skills based on how our parents, guardian, or
retaker modeled them for us and how we experienced them. Yet
w many of us have had at least one, if not both parents who had an
ue or childhood experience that negatively affected them.

s our childhood experiences along with our own unique
rsonalities, values, and beliefs that help shape our definition of
nat it means to be a parent. However, there is a low ceiling effect
re if this is all you are relying on to parent your best.

ame across a survey of parents of student athletes conducted by
. Richard Horowitz of Growing Great Relationships. In it, one of the
estions asked was where parents go to get advice and support for
renting. Out of all of the choices 80% said other parents. Now
n't get me wrong, it is always a good idea to be able to confide in
hers and ask for their advice. However, what works for another
mily will not always work for yours!

The challenge with any winning game plan, for sports or for your family in general, is that it takes much longer to design the plan than it does to execute it. Take for example an NFL team during the season. As soon as a game ends on Sunday, the coaching staff immediately gets to work on the game plan for the following week. Every day for the next seven days, the coaching staff is spending hours upon hours trying to design the best game plan in order to beat the other team in a sixty minute game. It is because of this lopsided tradeoff of planning hours versus minutes of playing that many families end up winging it.

If You Don't Have a Clear Game Plan

Being a parent is already hard enough, and adding sports to the equation can make it even more difficult. But if you want to be able to parent your best, then you must have a clear game plan in place.

Sports Parents without their own clear game plan typically experience the following:

- Struggle to find family balance
- Feel like they are always trying to just keep up
- Try to copy another family's game plan
- Often feel like they are trying to survive (avoid the loss) rather than succeed (go for the win)
- Feel disconnected in their relationships with their child and spouse

The three most common types of game plans tend to be focused on getting a college scholarship, the parents choosing the sport for the child, or the game schedule itself as the game plan. But if this is your only idea of a winning game plan, than you are missing out on the best part of being a Sports Parent! No matter what game plan you have in place, remember this...

ur child's game schedule and college showcase schedule is not the me as your family's game plan.

the end of the day, there is no single best family game plan when it mes to Sports Parenting as every family has different goals and has lifferent family rhythm. However, there is a framework that will rve as a foundation for success in any family game plan.

e 4 Critical Steps to Parent Your Best™

e following is adapted from a model created by Robert S. Hartman, e creator of formal axiology (the science of human value). I was st introduced to it back in 2007 by Dr. David Mefford and his rtner Vera, two of the world's leading authorities in this science d also very close friends. The beauty of this model is in its nplicity and progressive steps. In fact, I have used it in coaching aletes, parents, other coaches, and even consulting with businesses leadership and management across the world.

© 2010 Parent Your Best

Step 1- Discovery

How well do you know yourself and your own strengths and weaknesses? What type of lens or filter do you look through when you make decisions about yourself? How well do you truly know your child's strengths and weaknesses? These questions and others like them are the first step in Discovery which is about knowing yourself and knowing your child.

As a parent, it is easy to assume we know and understand our child since we have known them all of their lives! However, when we rely on assumptions and preconceived ideas of who a person is, these habits end up taking the driver's seat in the way we choose to relate and interact.

Parents also tend to communicate way more than actually connecting with their child. Communication is quick, simple, and takes very little time between two people. Think about it for a moment. How often do the following questions make up the bulk of your daily conversation with your child?

- *How was practice today?*
- *Was it tough?*
- *Did the coach play you at a different position?*
- *Did you score?*
- *Did you beat (insert name of teammate)?*
- *Did your coach finally teach you how to tackle?*
- *Did your coach show you how to throw a curve ball today? He doesn't know what he's doing.*

While some of these questions are obviously important, there is very little depth to them and they don't encourage further conversation and connection.

Truly connecting with your child takes time, energy, and being intentional. Even then, many parents find it difficult. For some

rents, lack of connection is due to a jam packed weekly schedule.
r others, it's because it is all about them and not their child. Or, it
n be out of fear, not wanting their child to truly know who they are
cause of a broken or embarrassing past.

ad a recent conversation with a father whose son was a high school
-star football player, yet the father had never played sports and
is embarrassed about the way he physically looked.   He would
rely go to games as he did not want to embarrass his son.
)wever, if he had only taken the time to connect, he would have
irned that his son did not care at all about that but wanted nothing
ore than to have his father come to his games. The dad put his own
eds ahead of his son's needs. Look what he missed.

ie of the keys to moving beyond communication and start
nnecting is the word *intimacy*. Now I am not asking the Sports Dad
ading this right now to be soft! But here is how I define the word:

In-to-me-see

here in your relationship with your child do you share intimacy?
ive you experienced those moments with your child that seemed to
)p time? These moments happen when you are able to look at each
her without judgment and see the other for who they really are and
t just for what they do.

scovery begins with prioritizing focused conversational time with
ur child on a daily basis, even if it's only for fifteen minutes. During
ur conversation, be aware of the words you use and the questions
at you ask during your time together. Also pay attention to how
ur child responds, not only for content, but for the feeling or
notion behind what is expressed. Remember, knowing yourself and
owing your child is about connecting, not just communicating.

Step 2- Acceptance

Have you ever heard of the saying that coaches tell athletes to *'choose your parents wisely'?* There is a lot of truth to this when talking about your child's athletic talent. However, the reality is that we don't get to choose our parents.

Maybe you were a highly gifted athlete yourself back in the day, or maybe there was not an ounce of athleticism in your body, yet your child loves to play sports. Either way, your child did not get to choose you when it comes to their athletic ability.

Let me ask you this...

When the game is on the line and your child performs poorly, maybe even has the worst game of his or her life; *do you choose your child?* In other words, do you choose your child and all of their imperfections regardless of their performance? Even more important, does your child know it?

Unfortunately for some Sports Parents, this step is conditional.

How often do you catch yourself comparing your child to other players on the team or to their older brother or sister? Or how about comparing your child to yourself if you had a successful athletic career? Choosing your child can become conditional when it's based on their performance, instead of unconditional when it's based on the person.

How About You?

When it comes to choosing yourself, do you fall into the trap of comparing who you are and what you have to other Sports Parents? The athletic body they have or used to have, the car they drive, the clothes they wear, the better school their child may go to with the better athletic program, or all of the top camps they send their child to all summer long? If you're not careful, you may end up trying to be

meone else - someone you were not meant to be. When you don't
oose to be your authentic self, your child knows it and this results
a connection struggle.

he Relationship Killer

hat happens when someone is on your team that you did not
oose? The natural tendency is to try and control them, make them
who you want them to be. If they can't or won't change to your
ing, the result is they are kicked off the team or viewed as an
tcast or outsider.

e same thing can happen when it comes to your relationship with
ur child. If it is based on control and what you want your child to
versus unconditionally choosing them for who they are, then your
ationship will suffer. So what's another option other than the
ntrol approach? *Using influence.*

**w do you influence your child or influence others who influence
ur child?**

starts with choosing your child no matter what, even if they
barrass you, anger you, or make extremely poor decisions. If your
ild feels accepted and chosen by you, no matter how well or poorly
ey play, you will gain influence over them. And the best part about
s is how your child will experience you, with unconditional love.

ditionally, you will not always be able to control what friends,
achers, and coaches your child interacts with. Therefore, taking a
lues-driven approach to influencing others will help to shape the
vironment that your child is in. For example, does your child hang
ound teammates who may be good players but seem to be lazy
hletes and unmotivated to work hard? Or how about having your
ild work with an outside coach or trainer to improve their
hleticism, but in truth they are providing more of a high priced
bysitting session and taking your money?

The take home point here is that influencing others who have influence on your child can take a lot of time and energy on your part, but making this a priority will dramatically affect your child.

Step 3- Growth

How often do you feel like you need to stay on your child and at times give them a hard push (even a big kick in the rear end) when it comes to getting better in their sport or improving their grades? Do you find yourself focusing all of your time and attention on your child's development to the exclusion of your own? Here are the three most common mistakes when it comes to developing yourself and your child.

The first mistake is not making yourself a priority in your weekly schedule. At least two or three times per week I hear from student athletes about how hard their parents push them and want them to improve, but they don't seem do anything for themselves. Coaches call it the 'do *as I say not as I do*' mentality.

The second mistake to growth and development is not being able to let go and allow your child make mistakes. You may feel you have made enough mistakes in the book in life, and therefore you don't want your child to go through what you did. But remember this...

Without risk, there is no growth. All people make mistakes, especially children, who are just learning how to deal with life. If they are punished for mistakes, they will be afraid to take a risk again, because they may fail. It is wise to discuss mistakes with your child openly and objectively, so they can learn and use them as stepping stones toward growth; without risk, there is no growth and no reward!

So who are you willing to risk to be there, for yourself and for your child?

It's okay to let them fail, in fact it is probably the only way they will actually learn. Just make sure you're right there if they need you to

lp them get back up without correcting their mistakes for them.
th of you will be better for it in the long run.

e last roadblock is the temptation to make excuses for your child.
hey hear you giving them a way to bail out, then they immediately
arn that they don't need self-accountability or self-responsibility.

**hen have you found yourself making excuses for your child's
ffering performance or poor decision making when it comes to
eir sport?**

ep 4- Celebration

s party time! What does celebrating with your child look like? How
es he or she prefer to celebrate? Is this different than the way you
e to celebrate? What do you actually celebrate? Why do you
lebrate? What has to happen to cause a celebration with your child
en it comes to their sport? These are just some of the many
estions that are important to answer before their season begins.

hile winning a tournament or a championship is definitely cause for
lebration, it isn't the only time or reason to celebrate.

an remember a time when growing up; I played in a tennis
urnament in Pensacola, Florida. While I didn't make it past the
ird round, one of my best friends ended up getting to the finals in
s age group for the first time. He got crushed by one of the top
eded juniors in the state of Florida, and instead of his parents
lebrating all of his hard work and effort to make it to the finals,
ey focused on what he did not achieve, the championship. Losing
esn't feel great, but it doesn't always have to feel horrible either.
fact, when you lose you can actually win! How? By taking what
u learned and applying it to future performances.

lebration that focuses solely on a successful performance result or
tcome can create a frustrating and pressure filled family
vironment.

Does this mean you should throw a big party every time your child does something well, shows improvement, or makes a big play in their game? Not at all. But on the flip side, maybe you're not celebrating enough.

Tom and Amy, two great friends of mine, took their seventh grade daughter through an exercise called the Connection Inspection Worksheet, which serves to help parents get a clearer perspective as to what their child wants when it comes to their sport and also uncovers any relationship barriers that the child is currently experiencing.

When Amy first asked their daughter to look at the items on the worksheet, she said that there was nothing on the list that really applied to her parents. But after nudging a few more times, their daughter finally revealed that she wished Tom and Amy supported her differently during her volleyball game.

What's funny is that Tom and Amy thought they were already supporting her in every way that they could. In fact, when Tom first heard his daughter's response, he couldn't believe it and was ready to list all of the ways he felt he completely supported her! Instead of defending his position, he asked her exactly how she would like them to support and celebrate during her game. Their daughter said that she wished her parents would yell and scream for her like her teammates' moms did. I only wish I could have been there in that moment to see the look on their faces!

So the next game, Tom and Amy played cheerleader, screaming loudly and praising her efforts which completely took them out of their comfort zone. Did I forget to mention that Tom is also the high school athletic director of the school?

The point of the story is that Tom and Amy thought they were supporting their daughter in the best way they knew how, but after directly talking about it using the Connection Inspection worksheet as a guide, they realized their daughter wanted support and celebration

look completely different. In the end, they both put their own
mfort levels aside to be who their daughter wanted them to be!

eware the Impact of Your Celebration

I mentioned in the introduction, over the past four years I have
d the opportunity to review over two thousand Ready To Play™
ental profiles of high school athletes looking at how an athlete
akes decisions in real time about themselves and the world around
em. While no surprise, two of the mental attributes that
nsistently showed lower clarity scores were self-esteem and self-
orth. **This is very important for you to know as it relates to
lebration. Young athletes often develop a false sense of self-
teem and self-worth because of the way their parents celebrate
d communicate *how* they value their child.**

s EVERY Sports Parent believes that their child has the potential to
the next athletic superstar, but constant and overly dramatic
lebration is the biggest contributor to your child's being unrealistic
out their abilities and what they can actually do. Then when they
ay poorly, they don't have the ability to cope or deal with failure.

e you familiar with the saying 'what gets rewarded gets repeated'?
ere are many ways to celebrate different levels of achievement,
complishments, and effort in your child's sport. One strategy that I
ve found to be successful is to give them an EARful whenever you
el the need. In other words, **recognize your child's:**

- **E**ffort
- **S**uccessful **A**ction
- **P**ositive **R**esult

ould encourage you to work through the *what, why, where, when,*
d *how* of celebration when it comes to your child's sports
perience by sitting down and sharing your thoughts with your child.
ur biggest celebration could just be one play away!

I would love to hear what, why and how you celebrate and recognize your child's athletic success. Let me know on the Facebook page Parent Your Best™.

The Parent Your Best™ Game Plan Workout

Okay, here is what I want you to do now. Get out a sheet of paper and work through the following questions on the next page. Or you can go online to www.parentyourbest.com/bookresources and download the worksheet for helping you develop your **Parent Your Best™ Defensive Strategy.**

---

1. *Summarize your overall philosophy and approach to Sports Parenting. (Have you actually ever written this out before?)*

2. *What about this approach is working well for you? What is missing from this approach that could be negatively affecting your relationship with your child and preventing a more positive experience for you both?*

3. *After reviewing the 4 Critical Steps to Parent Your Best™, which step needs the most attention right now? What would change in your relationship and Sports Parenting experience by working through this step?*

4. *What action step are you willing to take right now to address this step?*

Keys to Creating an Effective Game Plan

1. Be clear about who your family wants to be in sports & life

2. Be clear about what your family wants to achieve

3. Determine your core family values

4. Understand the demands of each family member's daily schedule

5. Understand and be aware of the individual qualities of each family member

agine if you applied this four step formula along with the five keys effective game plans to your own family game plan. How would ur relationship with your child be different?

the next chapter, you are going to find out how I quickly learned out Sports Parent Traps when I first started coaching, why you ould know what they are, and most importantly how to avoid em!

Ch.3- Parent Your Best™-
The Defensive Strategy

"It's not about protecting your child; it's about being more fully aware of your child."

st like in sports, as a Sports Parent, having the right defensive ategy can sometimes be your best offensive strategy. But how any times have you seen stories on the news of the crazy Sports rent who ends up in jail? Even when the altercation ended up ving nothing to do with the actual game itself? I had the portunity to be interviewed by WCNC-TV, the NBC television ition affiliate for the Charlotte, NC area, regarding this very kind of cident.

emale high school basketball player on the visiting team attempted walk over to the home team's side after her game was over and ring the start of the boy's high school basketball game. According the school district's rules, this was not allowed and a police officer spectfully told her to return back to the visitor's side. Seeing the ficer speak to his daughter, the girl's father came out of the eachers to see what the problem was. In the heat of the moment, e father ended up assaulting the police officer and the girl and her other joined in as well.

ily a week before that incident, a father of a high school basketball ayer was charged with assaulting his son's first year head basketball ach because he felt his son wasn't getting enough playing time.

Both of these dads made a public apology that included being regretful of their actions. They had the wrong defensive strategies as part of their game plan as a Sports Parent.

In July 2009, Sports Illustrated for Kids published the results of a study from over 1,000 kids across the United States asking various questions on their take on sports. The two results that caught my eye were the following:

- 42% of kids would like to participate in more sports

- 70% of kids have seen parents shout too loudly from the stands, and 32% of kids have seen parents argue with coaches

Again, here are more results that continue to point to the question from earlier chapters in this book. Are youth sports more about the parents or about the kids?

While these types of stories attract our attention and evoke a great deal of emotion, I am not as worried about those parents as I am concerned for you.   Specifically, I am referring to the invisible traps that go on in your family's daily life that you may not even be aware of.

Do you ever get frustrated when you see your child acting too lazy during a game? Or embarrassed when they make a poor decision? Or use bad technique that leads to a messed up play or losing a game? Does it drive you crazy? If you find yourself struggling with these types of issues, you may have fallen into a Sports Parent Trap.

So, just what is a Sports Parent Trap?

It is a roadblock that prevents you from being the BEST parent that you can be for your child right now. The worst part is that these traps are completely invisible. By yourself, you probably will never even see them coming!

ow do you fall into a Sports Parent Trap?

ere are a ton of different ways to get caught, but here are the top
n most common reasons in no particular order:

1. You want your child to succeed in ways that you never did.
2. You want your child to have what you never had.
3. You want your child to experience what you never did.
4. You want to make sure your child has an edge.
5. You believe your child is the next great professional athlete.
6. You expect your child to get a college athletic scholarship in return for all of the money you are pouring out into their sport.
7. Your older child is a great athlete, so why shouldn't your younger child be?
8. You want to be able to hang out with a certain social crowd and can do so by leveraging your child's successful performance.
9. You define your own self-worth based on the success of your child's performance.   If they play poorly, you're a bad parent.
10. The only way you know how to connect with your child is through competitive sport.

hile these tend to be more of the common ones, there is one not
ted that serves as the common denominator to all of them. It
pically presents itself in times of pressure, intense emotional
uations, or when decisions need to be made without much time. I
n talking about those conversations with your child that are built
ound *compliance*. For example, do any of the following phrases
und familiar?

- *I want you to make aggressive tackles and don't be scared to take shots in your game today!*

- *Why were you passing the ball out there today after we talked about how you should score more?*

- *I don't understand, why were you jogging around and looking lost? I told you that you need to be way more active in the beginning of the game.*

While you may have the best of intentions, it is the way you are communicating that hurts the relationship.

Commitment Trumps Compliance

If the majority of your communication with your child is what you want FROM them versus what you want FOR them, your relationship is built on compliance. When the focus of your communication is what you want FOR your child, then it simply becomes a matter of your choosing to commit to helping them reach their goals in a more supportive way.

What if you find yourself in a Sports Parent Trap?

First know that it is impossible to completely avoid these traps. We are all human and want the best for our kids. **However, what matters most is what you choose to do once you become aware that you are in one.**

Here are a few of the more common Sports Parent Traps along with a few suggested solutions that I have arrived at while working with student athletes and their parents.

   Correcting- When you watch your child play, do you constantly look to find faults in their performance, especially when it comes to a technical or tactical situation? Is this a bad thing? It is if you are constantly taking that information and communicating it to your child as if you were their coach. No matter how good your intent, this form of communicating almost always comes across as judgmental.

   Solution- If you do recognize faults in your child's performance, ask yourself *"How can I communicate this information in a way* *that will actually help my child play better?"* Another idea is to ask questions based on what you see rather than making judgmental statements. Without changing the way you communicate when it comes to correcting, your child will INSTANTLY feel like they are valued in their relationship with you based on their performance! Ask the question in a way that comes across as supportive and encouraging. For example, *"Don't worry about that turnover you made son, you obviously did not mean to do that. If you could go back and do it again, what would do differently?"*

Comparing- It is SO easy to get caught in this Sports Parent Trap. There are three main ways parents can provide comparative feedback- with other players, with siblings, or with themselves 'back when I used to play...' Yes I know you want your child to play better! However, taking this approach will again communicate to your child that you value them based on their performance.

Solution- So when is it OK to use comparative language? When the focus is a YOU vs. YOU approach instead of a YOU vs. THEM. In other words, when talking with your child, compare a poor performance with a time when you noticed they performed the same skill well. Or, you can always just leave that up to the coaches and simply support their having fun. Both ways work!

Controlling- Do you often find yourself telling your child exactly what to do? Telling them the decisions that they 'should' make on the field or court? When I go and watch my athletes play, I hear their parents tell them right before the game *"Okay, this is your big day Nick! Here is what I want you to go out there and do."*

While you may think you are getting them ready to play their best, you are actually paralyzing their decision making. Think about it, you are likely giving them four or five things to do or be aware of. Then, their coach tells them another four or five things to remember. No wonder so many of the youth games I get to watch start off so flat. Too many of these kids suffer from paralysis by analysis and not wanting to disappoint their parents or coach!

Solution- If you do feel it necessary to impart your timely wisdom, focus on only ONE thing. Just make sure that the one thing is not an outcome such as scoring two goals or rushing for over three hundred yards. If you do that, you will reinforce to your child that their self-worth is tied to their performance. I suggest to parents the following formula:

- **Praise their preparation-** *"You've practiced hard all week. How great is it to know that you are better today than you were only four days ago! I am excited to see the results of all of your hard work today out on the pitch!"*
- **Acknowledge & compare their strength-** *"I remember the last game when you used your speed to run on to the ball and serve it in for the game winning goal!"*
- **Plant a future seed-** *"I can't wait to see how you are going to use your speed today! Go out there, have fun, and be yourself!"*

Enabling- Do you serve as your child's personal assistant scheduling everything they do for them? Do you constantly have to remind your child to bring their cleats and equipment to practice? If your child forgets his cleats, do you run home to get them? Better yet, just go out and buy a new pair and rush back to the field? After practice, do you clean up after your child and his teammates?

Enabling happens when you consistently do something for your child when they are fully capable of doing it on their own. The result is that your child then learns that they don't have to be responsible and can always count on (use) you to get them out of a bind. Now you might be thinking *"but I don't want them to forget anything because I don't want to have to drive back home to pick up whatever it was they forgot!"* Well, ask yourself whose fault it is. You need to let them forget, make the mistake, and suffer the consequences! That's the only way your child will actually learn responsibility.

I can't tell you how many high school juniors and seniors that I work with have no idea of their own schedule! When trying to set a workout time and date, their response is always *"I don't know what my schedule is, can you call my mom?"* To which I immediately reply *"Are you kidding me? This is supposed to be YOUR sport right?"* In fact, it's because of this that when I work with high school athletes, all of the scheduling is done through them and not their parents! I still give the schedule to the parents so they are informed, but ask them not to be a constant reminder of their child's daily schedule. It's amazing when mom or dad pays for a training session that their teenage son forgot about. You tend to grow up really quickly after only doing that once!

Solution- Get a calendar and put it in a visible place in your house that both you and your child agree on. Schedule a 'team meeting' once a week with them and go over the weekly schedule. Better yet, during your meeting, have your child input their weekly schedule into their own cell phone calendar. This helps to further create accountability and responsibility in your child.

Blaming- When your son or daughter has a bad game, do you find excuses for them? Do you get embarrassed easily in front of other parents when this happens? During the game, do you lean over to the other dad or mom beside you and make up a reason for a poor decision or mistake by your child? Here are some of the more common excuses that I often hear:

- *Wasn't feeling good this morning*
- *Not used to playing in this kind of weather*
- *Needs new shoes*
- *Coach has him or her in a new position*

- *The other kid was playing dirty*
- *The coach did not communicate effectively*
- *The coach obviously plays favorites*
- *Your child was loaded up with homework last night*
- *Your child did not eat lunch today*
- *Your child RARELY plays like that, you don't know what's wrong*

Solution- Is it wrong or bad to give excuses? It is if you think your child's performance is a reflection of the quality of your parenting. Don't forget....IT'S JUST A GAME! Before you give an excuse to anyone about your child's performance, ask yourself the following questions:

- *Why do I feel like I owe this person an excuse?*
- *Does he or she directly determine playing time for my child?*
- *Do I find myself offering excuses for my child's poor performance before being asked by another parent?*

Entitlement- Out of all of the Sports Parent Traps mentioned, this one might be the most common of them all, at least in the United States. Why? Parents pay a whole lot of money for their child to play in club sports. In some cases over $3,000 per season! So when your child does not get treated fairly, get enough 'exposure' to college coaches, not enough playing time, or maybe doesn't get to play at all, it's no wonder parents get frazzled. The trap here is that if you are paying for it, you expect to see immediate tangible results!

However, it's not all your fault. Training young athletes is well over a $4 billion dollar industry. If your child is 'good enough', it seems that these clubs will promise you a college scholarship on a silver platter. Think of all of the various expenses that now come with just being able to play a competitive sport. From the lightest shoes to the newest titanium driver to attending every sports camp and combine possible just so your child will get that extra bit of exposure, the youth sports industry preys on parents knowing that you will be sure to come through for your child.

Solution- Be aware that just because you 'pay to play' doesn't mean that your child automatically gets to step up to the front of the line. Before enrolling your child in a club program, ask yourself the following questions:

- *What's the number one reason I want to enroll my child in this particular organization?*
- *Do they have an age appropriate developmental plan?*
- *What are the club's core values? Are these consistent with my family's core values?*
- *What can I expect to see differently in my child a year from now in terms of physical and skill development?*
- *Does the club value winning over development?*
- *What is the time commitment that will be required to participate? Is this realistic for our family?*
- *What additional resources are offered for parents?*
- *What are the rules and expectations that the club has for parents?*

Avoid the Traps but Watch Out for The Roadblocks

Now that you have learned about the top six Sports Parent Traps and how to deal with them, I want to share with you a few of the key roadblocks that can also get in the way of you being able to parent your best.

- Distortions- lack of understanding or clarity
- Dissonance- what you say is different than what you do
- Discouragement- devaluing your child
- Distractions- positive or negative actions or events that prevent concentration or divide one's attention
- Dilemmas- unforeseen negative situations

Like the Sports Parent Traps, these roadblocks tend to show up in our family lives every day. But just being aware of them can help you to keep a healthy relationship with your child.

The Ultimate Sports Parenting Question

There is one last question that I have found serves as a great litmus test when it comes to your relationship with your child. In fact, it is the #1 question EVERY Sports Parent should ask themselves on a daily basis. What is it?

"Who does (insert name) need me to be right now?"

The reason this is such a powerful question is because it helps you to keep your focus on the other person (your child) rather than on yourself. Remember, it's not always about you!

 *Try it out the next time you have a meaningful conversation and let me know what happens by sharing it on my Facebook page- Parent Your Best.*

The Parent Your Best™ Defensive Strategy Workout

Okay, here is what I want you to do now. Get out a sheet of paper and work through the following questions on the next page. Or you can go online to www.parentyourbest.com/bookresources and download the worksheet for helping you develop your **Parent Your Best™ Defensive Strategy.**

1. *List the top 3 Sports Parent Traps that you find yourself falling into. How is this affecting your relationship with your child?*

2. *What action step are you willing to commit to right now to address at least one of these traps?*

3. *Which of the Sports Parent Roadblocks do you struggle with the most? What impact is this having on your relationship with your child?*

4. *What action step are you willing to commit to right now to address this roadblock?*

5. *Putting yourself in your child's shoes, how is your child currently experiencing you in the following three environments? What effect does this have on their performance and love for the game?*

    a. *During the week/at family dinner*
    b. *During the game*
    c. *During the ride home from the game*

6. *How can you begin to improve each of these environments?*

7. *What do you want FROM your son or daughter when it comes to their participation in youth sports? (List 3 things)*

8. *What do you want FOR your son or daughter when it comes to their participation in youth sports? (List 3 things)*

Ok, now for the BIG TWIST...

Although worded a little differently, have your child answer these same questions based on what <u>they</u> think and how <u>they</u> are currently experiencing you.

Be sure you communicate to your child that their answers WILL NOT BE JUDGED as good or bad, but instead will be used as a catalyst for conversation that will serve to improve your relationship as a family both on and off the field, court, or ice.

1. *List the top 3 Sports Parent Traps that you feel your parents fall into when it comes to YOUR sport and the effect it is having on you. (refer to p.48)*

2. *What would your family life look like if these traps were non-existent? How would our relationship be different? How would it affect your performance in your game?*

3. *How are you currently experiencing your parents in the following scenarios as it relates to your sport?*

    a. *During the week/at the dinner table*
    b. *During the game*
    c. *During the car ride home after the game*

4. *What do you like about how your parents communicate with you in each of those three scenarios?*

5. *What would you like to see happen differently in each of those three scenarios? How would this affect your performance and love for the game?*

Want some help working through these questions?

If you are anything like me, completing questions at the end of a chapter can actually be challenging to do on your own. Why? It's too easy and tempting to just quickly answer each question without a lot of focused thought.

If you would like to have some help and really get clear on your answers check out the Parent Your Best Game™ or the Parent Your Best™ Bootcamp at www.parentyourbest.com. In fact, get a special discount code in the online resource area for this book!

Being aware of the Sports Parent Traps and the Roadblocks to parenting your best is a great defensive strategy to add to your family game plan when it comes to sports. Imagine if your entire family got together twice per month for the next three months and discussed if your child was experiencing any of these traps or roadblocks? How would this change your family's sports culture?

In the next chapter, I will share with you a few great offensive strategies for parenting your best. Keep reading if you want to find out the truth about things like respect and accountability!

Ch.4 Parent Your Best™ - The Offensive Strategy

"One of the best offensive strategies for parenting your best is built on the concept of modeling; what you are asking from your child you are asking of yourself."

Do you feel like you have to keep a competitive edge when it comes to being a Sports Parent? Always trying to make sure to position your child for the best chance of athletic success? In sports, the goal of an offensive strategy is to put the team in a position to score the most points in order to win the game. However, as a Sports Parent, an offensive strategy means putting yourself in the position to be the parent that your child needs you to be.

Offensive Strategies That Don't Work

An area that tends to generate the most tension between a parent and their child are conversations focused on the child's performance. For example, have you witnessed a parent telling their child right after a game or practice things they should do for a better performance the next time? Here a few phrases I recently heard attending a U-16 boys' lacrosse game and a U-15 girls' soccer game:

- *"Why did you make that decision that caused the turnover? You should have done what I would have done and rolled out the other way."*

- *"You were too slow out there today; we've got to work on getting faster."*

- *"No wonder you keep getting beat by your man, you're too out of shape."*

- *"Your coach doesn't have you in the wrong position honey. You're fit enough; you just need to lose a few pounds."*

And what's the usual reaction and facial expression of their child? It's definitely not a huge smile and a response saying *'Thank you so much for bringing that to my attention! Can I start working on those things right now?'* Instead, these types of statements invite complete silence or a verbal attack back at mom or dad.

How about when parents try to persuade their child to improve physical fitness using guilt by saying *'Your mother and I pay a lot of money so that you can participate on this travel team and this is how you choose to respond?'* Or how about my all time favorite *'You keep saying that you want to get better. Your father goes out and buys you some new weights (training equipment), but I don't see you doing anything.'*

Maybe you know parents whose definition of encouragement is to withhold something that the child wants until they have finished practicing a specific skill i.e. 200 free throws in the backyard or completed a two mile run to get fit.

How about you? Do you find yourself using any of these offensive strategies such as guilt, withholding, or shame when trying to get your child to improve their physical performance?

Have there been times when you feel like your child doesn't show you respect or appreciation for all the things you do and provide for them when it comes to helping them get better? When we aren't given the respect we think we deserve, we often try to demand it.

Do you ever feel like you sacrifice more for your child's sport than they do when it comes to working on getting better on their own time? It doesn't take much to get frustrated when over a reasonable period of time their work ethic and self- motivation doesn't match your expectations for their development. When this happens, do you respond by telling them what you accomplished at their age?

It's easy to get frustrated when you are spending a ton of money on your child and sacrificing all of your time for their sport and they don't show respect or display the effort and hard work to get better. But before you are ready to snap, step back and assess where in your own life you are currently modeling the attitude and behavior you want your child to display. If you aren't, than the 'do what I say not what I'm doing' mentality only creates more tension and pressure between the two of you. Why? Creating experiences of dissonance with your child, when what you say is different than what you do, doesn't help them get better, in fact it can encourage them to quit!

There is one last strategy I haven't mentioned that that can be used with your child that when misapplied, creates instant tension and a sea of negative emotions. It is a word that tends to be used only when all else fails and disappointment in your teenager's choices relative to your values and expectations are at an all-time high. Can you guess what I am referring to? *Accountability*.

Have you ever used accountability as a punishment with your child when it comes to their sports experience? If so, what did that conversation look like? What was the result? My bet is that the both of you parted ways feeling frustrated, mad, and emotionally toxic.

What does Accountability look like in your family?

Using accountability as a punishment teaches your child that accountability really means following the rules and it is something that is put in place to control their behavior. You may view this as an offensive strategy, but your child will perceive it differently and become defensive. Accountability has limited value as an offensive strategy when you choose to use it as a punishment.

If you struggle with any of the offensive strategies such as guilt, withholding, shame, or the misuse of accountability, the good news is that there is a healthier way to influence your child and their desire to get better.

The #1 Offensive Strategy for Sports Parents

One of the most difficult and challenging things to do in order to parent your best is to make sure that your needs are not always secondary to your child's needs. In fact, the only way that you can give yourself the best opportunity to consistently parent your best is to apply the principle:

Live Well Before Your Parent Well

In other words, take care of yourself first. If you don't, then you simply can't be the best parent that your child needs you to be.

I am sure you have told your child that if they are stressed out, mentally exhausted, and physically tired all of the time then they can't expect to perform well. But guess what? The same thing applies to you when it comes to your ability to parent your best!

How can you desire respect from your child if you don't respect yourself when it comes to taking care of your own body, mind, and spirit?

 *What offensive strategies as a Sports Parent have you found to be successful? Let me know by sharing it on my Facebook page- Parent Your Best.*

The Parent Your Best™ Offensive Strategy Workout

One of the best offensive strategies for parenting your best is the concept of modeling and that what you are asking from your child you also ask of yourself. Are you showing your child that you respect your own health and well-being? What does self-accountability look like when it comes to taking care of you?

Okay, here is what I want you to do. Get out a sheet of paper and work through the following questions. Or you can go online to www.parentyourbest.com/bookresources   and   download   the worksheet for helping you develop your **Parent Your Best™ Offensive Strategy.**

- How do you currently show your child that you respect yourself in body, mind, and spirit? In what way does this encourage and model for your child their own desire for self-improvement?

- What does your child see that you hold yourself accountable for when it comes to the principle of 'Live well before you parent well'? If you slide when it comes to taking care of yourself, what message does that send to your child in terms of how they should value themselves?

- Write down your number one bad habit that you are willing to break starting today. By erasing this bad habit from your daily routine, who would this allow you to be, and what would this allow you to do and have differently and better in your life?

- Challenge your child to do this activity with you for the next thirty days.

One Final Thought...

Taking care of yourself is a championship offensive strategy for parenting your best and a great way to model for your child the values and behaviors you want to instill in them. However, be aware that you don't have to have a lean and athletically sculpted body in order to do so!

Simply starting off by walking or jogging twenty minutes a day sets a wonderful example for your child. Remember, they don't always listen to you but they are always watching you.

If you would like to have some help or want some advice on becoming more physically fit check out the Parent Your Best Game™ or the Parent Your Best™ Bootcamp at www.parentyourbest.com. Also, I have included some great fitness resources in the online resource area for this book!

So imagine if in the next thirty days you kicked your number one bad habit and achieved the fitness result you desired?

- What example would this set for your child?
- How would they experience you differently?
- How would this reshape your personal and family values?

In the next chapter, you are going to learn the number one principle in human performance that applies to both you and your child when it comes to being your best!

Ch.5 Parent Your Best™- Effective Decision Making

"Make better decisions...get better results."

Have you ever looked back on a particular experience with your child and thought to yourself that maybe you didn't make the best decision with them or for them at the time? The bulk of my conversations with Sports Parents include not wanting to be too pushy, not wanting their child to be left behind, or they want to position their child for the best chance of athletic success.

 Ultimately, all of the decisions that you make are based on your values. These are what shape your self-identity as a Sports Parent. For example, see if you can figure out what is the core value that is driving the decision of the parent in the statements below:

- The parent who wants success much more than their child during a game

- The dad who sits or stands at the opposite end of where all of the other parents are sitting during the game

- Parents that are over-protective of their child and don't want them to ever get hurt

- Parents who enroll their child in every camp and clinic offered only to see their child get burned out in their sport

- The parent who constantly focuses on amount of playing time

- The parent who tells their kid it's okay to be selfish and score

Once the values are realized, then you can get a better understanding of how your value system and your decisions directly affect your capacity as a Sports Parent.

Think about it, how have your values and decisions significantly impacted yourself and your child's sports experience? Do any of the following apply to you?

Control

- Controlling where your child will attend or play sports in college
- Making a decision about your child's sports experience with the intention of raising your own social status

Fear

- Making a decision you may not normally make because you fear being judged by other sports parents
- The fear of not being good enough for your child because maybe you were not an athlete

Conflicts

- Switching schools, clubs, or coaches because it was you that had the issue rather than your child
- Pushing your child much harder than your spouse or partner
- Valuing sports completely differently than your spouse/partner or your child

Parents are preventing themselves from parenting their best when they don't take the time to reflect on the impact of their decisions and think clearly through the WHY of their decisions.

The #1 Secret Known by Elite Athletes

When working with an athlete's mindset, the core of mental performance starts with what you believe and how you feel about yourself. In fact, the Ready To Play™ mental performance program that I use with my athletes starts with the following guiding principle:

You can't outperform or outlive your own self-identity

This same principle applies to you as a Sports Parent. Your capacity to parent begins with WHAT you believe and value about yourself, as well as HOW you value yourself and your child. For example, if you never played sports at a competitive level growing up, then your self-identity as a Sports Parent might take the role of being a supporter and fan of your child or possibly even being completely disengaged from their sports. If you were an all-star MVP growing up and played sports in college, then your self-identity is likely to take the role of coach or sports agent in your relationship with your child. If you were a team player growing up, than your self-identity may take the shape of being a teammate with your child.

Think back for a moment on your own experience in sports and what your relationship was like with your own parents. Maybe you had an overactive parent that pushed you too hard or a parent that had absolutely nothing to do with sports? Or possibly you could be one of the lucky ones that look back and feel like your youth sports experience was like a fairy tale. Whatever your personal and situational past encompasses, those experiences, feelings, behaviors, and values strongly influence your current decision making process about sports and your own child.

Take a moment and reflect on your own childhood sports experience. How did that shape your current belief and decisions you make about

Sports Parenting? What values and opinions did you form about sports as a child?

 *How did your own childhood sports experience shape your current self-identity? Let me know by sharing it on my Facebook page- Parent Your Best.*

Have You Heard Of This Little Known Science?

Since becoming a performance coach in 1996, I have tried to pare down all of the different components of performance into just one single phrase. In 2005 I was introduced to a little known science that finally gave me the insight into how athletes, coaches, and parents make decisions. In fact, it is the mantra that now serves as the basis for all of my programs for athletes, coaches, and parents:

Make Better Decisions...Get Better Results™

As I have mentioned in earlier chapters in this book, the science is called *Formal Axiology,* the science of human value, and has been adapted into what is now known as *Sports Axiology™*. According to Dr. David Mefford, the world's leading authority in the science of formal axiology, it is best described as:

"...the mathematically-based science of evaluative judgment that objectively identifies how our mind analyzes and interprets our experiences as meaningful. It identifies how we are most likely to react in any given situation. It helps us to understand how people judge the "worth" of objects, people, systems, and the patterns we use to make judgments about anything. In turn, this allows us to translate these qualities into quantitative measurements which can then be compared, understood, and applied to our daily world."

Formal Axiology provides an excellent framework for decision making for Sports Parents. It divides decision making into three dimensions of value: systemic (mental/rational), extrinsic (physical/appearance-based), and intrinsic (emotional). In other words, there are three different ways that we can give meaning to an object, person, or event.

For example, let's use a shoe. Systemically, the mind can identify it either as a shoe or some other object that is not a shoe. Extrinsically, a shoe could be a soccer cleat, a specific kind of shoe that serves a specific practical purpose. Or, if it's a Nike soccer cleat, then that could be the best soccer cleat compared to all other soccer cleats. The extrinsic compares <u>this</u> shoe to the class of all shoes. Intrinsically, think of your child's favorite pair of soccer cleats. There is no other pair like it in the world! Refer to the chart below for a more detailed explanation of the three dimensions of value.

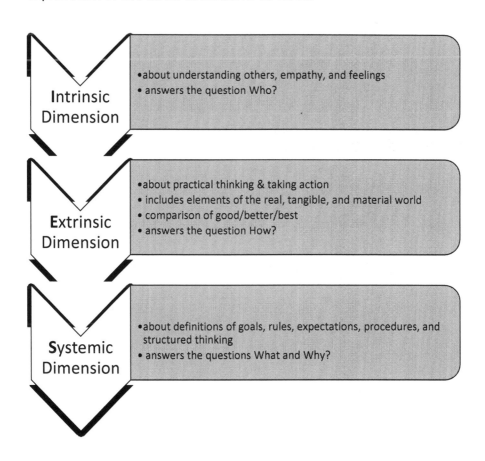

Intrinsic Dimension
- about understanding others, empathy, and feelings
- answers the question Who?

Extrinsic Dimension
- about practical thinking & taking action
- includes elements of the real, tangible, and material world
- comparison of good/better/best
- answers the question How?

Systemic Dimension
- about definitions of goals, rules, expectations, procedures, and structured thinking
- answers the questions What and Why?

Most parents are dominant in one or possibly two of these dimensions as their filter for making decisions. For example, phrases focusing on what you want FROM your child such as *'did you; you should have; what were you; why did you'* are systemic and are more focused on communication with your child than connecting conversation. On the other hand, a parent who tends to focus solely on having the best of everything (equipment, coaches, programs, players) and are competitive themselves are extrinsically driven. While the parent who focuses on the child first, the feelings they have, and the unique qualities about them, are more intrinsically driven.

Many Sports Parents tend to be extrinsically dominant during and after a game focusing on the child's performance, thus losing sight of the bigger picture (systemic) as well as being aware of what their child is experiencing during the game (intrinsic). A good example of this took place during the 2006-2007 soccer season when the Minnesota Youth Soccer Association took a survey of players, parents, and coaches. Below are some of the results as reported from their website www.mnyouthsoccer.org:

✓ *MYSA athletes report the following experiences:*

- 34% have been yelled at or teased by a fan.

- 15% report their parents get angry when they play poorly.

✓ *MYSA parents report the following experiences:*

- 90% report that people on the sidelines "never" or "almost never" distract athletes from focusing on the game.

- 26% report people "never" or "almost never" coach from the sidelines (meaning 74% do witness coaching

by adults other than an official coach from the
sidelines.)

✓ *MYSA Coaches report the following experiences:*

- 6% report they "never" hear coaching by other adults
from the sidelines (meaning 94% do hear coaching
from the sidelines.)

✓ *So what is Really Going On?*

- It is likely that parents perceive that "coaching from
the sidelines" is not distracting to their children.
Children tell a different story.

As you can see from this survey, the parents were making decisions
based on an extrinsic perspective (focusing on performance) not
realizing or taking into consideration how their children were
experiencing them (the intrinsic dimension).

The goal for making good decisions then is to consider all three value
dimensions when making choices that impact you and your family.
This way, you can then decide which dimension is most important to
apply to the situation at any given time.

*Note: For more information on the application of Sports Axiology in
parenting, coaching, or sports performance refer to the appendix in
this book.*

The Parent Your Best™ Decision Making Workout

Effective decision making as a Sports Parent begins with
understanding that values drive the process. Determining *what* you
value and how you make value judgments impacts what you believe
and the decisions you make about yourself and about your family.

Okay, here is what I want you to do. Get out a sheet of paper and
work through the following questions. Or you can go online to

www.parentyourbest.com/bookresources and download the
worksheet **Parent Your Best™ Decision Making Workout.**

- List Your Top 5 Core Family Values

  Write them down separately and then have each family
  member share what they wrote down

- Discuss what each particular core value looks like at home,
  at practice, and during the game

- What's the best version of what you look like as a Sports
  Parent at home and during a game?

- What's the best version of what your family looks like
  during a game? (discuss with your child)

- What's unique about your family when it comes to sports?
  (discuss this with your child)

- Complete the Sports Parent Mindset worksheet to find out
  HOW you value yourself and the world around you, and
  how this shapes your pattern of decision making as a
  Sports Parent

- Share with your child what your relationship was like with
  your own parents growing up when it came to sports.
  Discuss both the positive and negative experiences that
  you had and how this has influenced your own decision
  making as a sports parent

Workout Notes:

- Realizing that your Core Values list is different from your spouse's and your child's will help to understand why tension can occur in the most simple of family discussions

- Creating your list of Core Values can serve as a litmus test for decision making for both you and your child. This can be a great resource to refer to during discussions, because then the conversation doesn't have to be about you versus your child.

If you want a more exciting way to work through these exercises, be sure and check out the Parent Your Best Game™. It takes all of the questions, exercises, and actions in this book plus more and uses the language of sports along with a scorecard to help you Parent Your Best™ in an interactive and high-energy online environment.

Imagine if you decided to make it a priority to understand your own self-identity as a Sports Parent, how would that affect your family life? How could this "New You" affect the way you make decisions about yourself and your child when it comes to sports?

In the next chapter, I am going to share with you a life-changing motto that will definitely help you to parent your best!

Ch.6 Parent Your Best™-
The Partnership

*"Parents are teachers but they should also be students.
What is your child teaching you?"*

Has anyone ever asked you what YOU want your role to be as a Sports Parent? When it comes to a parent's role in sports, I have heard everything from being a fan, a manager, a sports agent, an owner, a teammate, and a coach. The truth is that a Sports Parent in today's landscape of competitive youth sports probably has to be a little of them all. Therefore, the role of a Sports Parent is more like a partnership. As their partner, how are you helping your child navigate through various issues such as dealing with pressure, self-esteem, self-confidence, developing their potential, and most importantly having a fun and enjoyable sports experience?

Typically schools and youth clubs hold their annual parent meeting to go over the rules that parents are expected to follow for the season. This is their attempt to control parental behavior during games and define your role for you. Unfortunately, in every parent meeting I have attended, the focus is on the WHAT NOT TO DO, and tips for HOW to be a great Sports Parent are rarely mentioned.

More importantly, it is what happens in daily life between the parent and their child beyond the game that should be a bigger focus, during the game and after the game merely reveals the health of their relationship with their child.

I see red flags when I go watch one of my athletes play and I hear comments from parents before the game like *"We have to get a win today"*, or after the game *"We just did not play well and looked tired."* For the most part statements like these are made out of excitement, passion, and support for their child; however in reality these statements create a pressure-filled environment. For example, I once heard one of my players respond to his father's comment about the team needing to play well before the game by saying *"Dad, are you going to strap up and play with us out there today?"*

On another occasion, I had the opportunity to train a high school athlete who was one of the best on the team and whose goal was to play in college. This player had grown up around the sport as one of his parents happened to be a successful former professional athlete. When we first began training, this player would occasionally throw up during a workout and say it was due to some bad food. However, after a few weeks, I put together that this happened only when the parent would come and watch the workout. Can you imagine the stress and pressure this athlete felt on a daily basis without his parent realizing the cause?

In his book *Until It Hurts*, author Mark Hyman discusses our obsession with youth sports and the negative effects it has on kids. He makes the statement that *"so much of what goes on around youth sports tempts and disarms us, distorting our judgment"* and that *"youth sports are not meant to serve as mere entertainment and leverage for adults"*.

(Note: If you want to hear an audio interview I did with Mark when his book was first released back in 2009 go to the resources link for this book at www.parentyourbest.com/bookresources)

What does a partnership with your child look like?

USA Swimming posted a very interesting article on their site titled 'How Parents Affect Success: An Athlete's Perspective'. The article was about a youth club in Texas that asked their swimmers about their parents. Think of your own Sports Parenting role as a partner as you read some of the following results:

12-14 Year Old Swimmers (Pre-Senior II Practice Group)

Things they love and appreciate:

- I like that my parents really enjoy the sport of swimming.
- I like that you take the time out of your day to take me to practice and meets.
- I like that you spend money on something I can have a future in.
- I like that my parents don't put pressure on me.
- I like how my parents support/care for me no matter what.
- I like when they make me feel better when I add time.
- I love that my parents want me to be my best.
- I love when my parents don't coach me.

Things they don't like:

- I dislike that my parents are never satisfied with my swims.
- I don't like when they don't understand you just don't drop every meet, even if my strokes look better.
- I dislike when they doubt my commitment.
- I dislike when my parents say I did badly; I am disappointed enough in myself already.
- I hate that my parents don't realize how hard I work to keep them happy.
- I hate when my parents only look at how well I do in my meets and not in practice.
- I hate that my parents have never been a swimmer, but they try to change and put down my swimming.
- I dislike when my parents get upset when I didn't get a cut even though I dropped time.
- Don't appreciate my effort when I do well.
- Don't buy healthy food for meets.
- I hate when my parents try to fix my strokes.

- I don't like when you try to make my goal times for me.

Can you identify with any of the statements above in your own relationship? Don't get me wrong, it is completely normal to get frustrated and emotional when these situations occur. But it is how you choose to respond to them that is most important. When you allow your emotions to get the best of you, your child can learn that your love for them is conditional.

Does your child only feel loved when they feel like they have impressed or pleased you? Do you react dramatically different with your child after a game when they have played hard, had fun, and gave it their best effort (even if they or their team lose) versus if they were the reason that their team won?

Your relationship with your child suffers the most when they feel your love for them is threatened, especially when you don't even realize it.

Building a House of Champions

In the fall of 2010 I created a seminar for parents and student athletes called 'Building a House of Champions'. The whole purpose of this interactive seminar is to educate parents on the importance of emotional literacy and the need for a healthy relationship with their child.

The theme for the event is *'Together I'll Play Better™',* as if your child is saying this to you. Notice the phrase is not Together We'll Play Better. It's not your sport. The main emphasis is on the word *Together,* in other words the healthier your relationship is between you and your child, the better they will play THEIR game. It's about being a partner with your child, not a teammate, agent, or coach. Think about this theme and how it relates to your relationship with your child. What specifically comes to mind?

How can you improve this concept of *Together*?

The first step is to determine if your relationship currently focuses more on communication than connection. When your focus is more about what you want FROM them than FOR them – you are stuck in communication. It is important to realize there is a huge difference between what you want them to do and how you want them to feel. They are both necessary, but the question to ask yourself is which space do you live in the most with your child?

When it comes to being a partner with your child in their sport, be aware that the experiences that you create, those moments of communication and connection, shape the beliefs that others (your family, other parents, and your child's coach) have about you and HOW they value you.

 *How does the 'Together I'll Play Better' motto show up in your own family life? Let me know by sharing it on my Facebook page- Parent Your Best.*

The Parent Your Best™ Partnership Workout

The best way to be a championship partner with your child is to fully embrace the *Together I'll Play Better*™ perspective as a Sports Parent.

Okay, it's time for you to figure out what communication and connection looks like in your own family by answering the questions below. Or you can go online to: www.parentyourbest.com/bookresources and download the worksheet **Parent Your Best™ Partnership Workout.**

- Complete the **Connection Inspection** worksheet found in the online resources area for this book.

- Have your child complete the **Connection Inspection** worksheet in the ways that they might be experiencing you.

- How often do you find yourself getting overly frustrated when it looks like your child is being lazy or shows a lack of effort in their game?

- How do you typically react when a referee makes a bad call against your child or your child's team?

- What does your conversation look like with your child after the game when they have disappointed you and not met your expectations for them?

- What's your body language and facial expression like when your child screws up a totally routine play that they make nine out of ten times?

- How are the experiences that you are creating in the way that you connect with your child shaping your family's culture?

- Are these experiences consistent with your core values?

Cont'd.

- What experience or series of experiences do you need to create in order to influence your child's belief about your relationship?

- How does your child experience your love kinesthetically (feeling & touch), visually (body language & facial expressions), and verbally in the following three environments?

    At home- To & from Practice- During games

- How do you define Parenting Excellence?

- How does your child define Parenting Excellence?

On Being a Partner with Your Child

The statements found in the Connection Inspection worksheet serve as warning signs to help you know when your partnership with your child might be in trouble. Below are some signs that your partnership with your child is positive and healthy:

- Remain calm when your child doesn't play well
- Encourage your child and their team no matter what
- Be honest with your child about their performance if they ask
- Keep a healthy distance from being too involved in your child's sports life
- Remember that it is just a game
- Emphasize your child's development over winning
- Model core values

- Show unconditional love
- Provide an emotionally stable home environment
- Comment on performance and effort over outcome
- Hold your child accountable and responsible
- Allow your child the freedom to fail
- Teach and model good decision making skills
- Focus on friendships and relationships that sports offers
- Show trust in the coach
- Create opportunities for your child

On Parenting Excellence

Striving for parenting excellence plays a huge role in your being a partner with your child in their sports experience. Below are my 6 E's of Parenting Excellence that can serve as a guide for you in parenting your best. They can also serve as a framework for Athletic Excellence to share with your child.

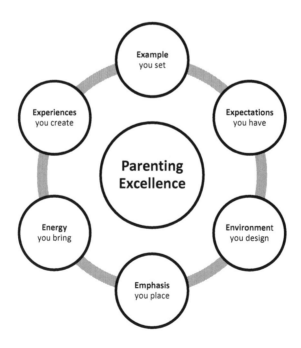

Gray Cook, one of the top sports physical therapists in the world, once made the statement to me during a rehab session with one of my athletes that 'the language of movement is through feel.' I would take this one step further and say that the language of life and relationships is through feel. If you want to be a great partner and support for your child, focus more on connection and less on communication - you both will be better for it.

In the next chapter, I am going to share with you a letter from a dad to his son and the impact it can have in your own family story.

Ch.7 Parent Your Best™- Your Story

"The best version of you is a blessing for your child."

What story do you tell your children about your own childhood sports experience with your family? What story are you currently telling now as a Sports Parent? The story that I commonly see is unintentionally wrapped in a blanket of conditional love and involves parents who want the best for their child, hope they will experience athletic success, strives to give their child opportunities that they never had, and looks to help their child gain a competitive edge.

 If any of these statements resonate with you and what you are experiencing right now in your relationship with your child, then ask yourself, is this the story I want to look back on and tell ten or twenty years from now?

Even if only parts of this story may be true in your family life, my hope for you after reading this book is that your story will be different and in a very positive way, like the story that follows.

The Letter from A Father

One day I was having a conversation with a close friend of mine, Jim Jordan, about Parent Your Best™ and he asked if I had ever read the letter that Steve Mariucci's father had written to the local newspaper when he was graduating from high school. Steve is a well respected former NFL Player and NFL Head Coach who currently is on the NFL Network.

My search for this letter led me to a conversation with Bob Johnson, the editor for the Milwaukee Wisconsin Journal Sentinel. It turned out that Steve's father, Ray Mariucci, was Bob's middle school teacher back when he was a boy! I could hear the excitement in his voice when I ask him about the letter written from Ray about Steve. What a great parent and teacher he must have been.

The letter was dated June 6, 1973 and the introduction from the editor stated "Today's editorial is a moving letter from a father to his high school athlete son, penned by an Iron Mountain resident who prefers that his name not be made public."

Dear Son:

I suppose a boy your age often wonders how he stacks up in the eyes of his dad. If my eyes have not already told you, perhaps I can express my feelings in this letter at the expense of some considerable over-emotion and sentimentalism.

How can I adequately express the feeling of pride I have for you not only as an athlete in uniform but as an individual out of it – the pride that is built up over a period of years in your dedication to athletics?

You've outgrown me by a couple of inches now, but it seems like yesterday that you sat on my lap watching the games on T.V. I explained the games to you then – now you explain them to me. Through the years I kept my eye on you. I've watched you develop, grow, and participate, and I've noticed many things...

I watched you devote your life to rigid training and clean living. I have seen you develop into a boy with spirit, confidence, and a will to win. Yet, along with this grew modesty, humility, and respect for the other guy along with a compassion for fellow players.

I've seen you cry and suffer silently in defeat and exalt in victory. There was no need to look at me in embarrassment when you thought you did not perform well, but I knew you always did the best you could.

And yet, there were the many times your play was outstanding – the homerun to win the ball game, the winning bucket, the second effort for the touchdown, and the final spurt to win the race. At times, I cried too – but with tears of pride.

I've seen you get a few knocks – at times helped off the field. And I've seen signs of pain on your face. I felt that pain too, my son. We used a lot of liniment nursing you through your aches and pains.

I've swelled with pride when the crowd gave you a standing ovation in appreciation of your efforts and performance. And how proud I was to be your father after a coach's comment, "He's the kind of son I would like to have!"

Then the compliments from different walks of life – the dentist with questions about next week's game and the grocer inquiring about your health. I've seen your mother's looks of pride, and I've heard your brothers and sisters boast about you.

You've earned these compliments, Son, not only with your fine efforts, but with your sportsmanship. I've seen you place yourself in the doorway of the opposing players' locker room to shake their hands – in victory or defeat – and I've heard you pass a few kind words to your opponent's coach. Never once have I seen you deliberately try to hurt an opponent or take advantage of an unfair situation. With all of this, you have earned the respect of coaches, officials, and opposing players.

Your concern and compassion for your teammates also show what a heartwarming scene – in the middle of the court, your arm around a sobbing teammate who had just missed a crucial free throw in a championship game!

I've never seen you grandstand. Yet, I've seen outstanding teamwork and sacrifice on your part that has helped your team to victory.

I've learned from you, Son – about courage, loyalty, and fair play –
and I admire your optimism and your philosophy of life. All in all, you've made my life richer and more meaningful. For this I thank you.

I'm also grateful for the many rich shared experiences, the thrills and memories and the feeling of pride when you're standing by my side, grateful for the absence of the phone calls from the police station or the hospital.

You may have a couple of broken bones and a few bumps and bruises for souvenirs, Son, but you also have a collection of a few trophies, medals, and newspaper clippings along with your established character to remind us that all of this was not in vain.

It isn't that important whether you make All Conference or Most Valuable. The point is that up to now you've played well and lived well – a step toward desirable and successful manhood. To say I'm proud of you, Son, is putting it mildly!

Love,
Your Dad

After reading this letter, what are some of the first thoughts that run through your mind? Have you written a letter like this before to your child? If not, what would want your letter to say?

The Power of Your Story

All of us can sum up any part of our lives in just a matter of sentences. For example, if I were to ask you to tell me about your own childhood sports experience you could do so in less than two minutes. But within those two minutes, what are you telling me about your life? What emotions are you sharing and what life experience did you gain?

Parent Your Best™- Your Story Workout

Think about your own story now as a Sports Parent. What story do you want to be able to tell? A great model to use as a foundation for telling your story is based on the 3 G's:

- **Grounded** in the truth

- **Guided** by your love and trust

- **Grown** through your relationships

Okay, now it's time to think about the story that **you** want to tell from this point forward as a Sports Parent. Go online to www.parentyourbest.com/bookresources and download the worksheet **Parent Your Best™- Your Story Workout.**

Your story can be found in your daily agenda, the goals you have, and the results you strive for. Evaluate an entire week's agenda and complete the following:

- Determine the actual number of contact hours you had with your child (I call these *Influential Hours*). How were they spent? What was the outcome?

- Describe the way you valued your child during each of these experiences focusing on who they were, what they did, what they were thinking.

- List your top three most influential results.

- What impact did it have on your child?

- How did this shape their belief about you? About their sports experience? Are you OK with this?

- Is there anything that you would have done differently? If so, how would this change your desired result?

- Write a similar letter to your child like the one written to Steve Mariucci from his father (but you don't have to actually send it to your local newspaper). How would you use this letter to speak to and influence your child's life? To paint a picture of their possible future using their God-given talents? After you write the letter, put it away and review it each year until your child graduates from high school; then give it to them as a gift of love.

Here's the great news! No matter if your story so far is a fairy tale or an action-packed drama - it's not over yet. And that means starting right now, you get to choose the ending that you want it to have in terms of the role you want to play and what you want your relationship with your child to be based upon. Like all inspirational stories, there are times of trial and tribulation, but that's where life happens. Without those times, there would be little reason to truly celebrate the good stuff.

 *I would love to hear your story! Let me know by sharing it on my Facebook page- Parent Your Best.*

Parent Your Best™- The Next Step

"This is not the end, but rather the beginning of your journey of what it takes to parent your best."

In 2001 and 2003 I had the opportunity to work with the Atlanta Beat, one of the eight original teams in the Women's United Soccer Association. This was a pivotal time in my own coaching career as the experience I gained from working with the head coach Tom Stone was second to none. At that time he was one of the few soccer coaches in the United States that valued Sports Performance training which allowed me to work WITH him and not just FOR him.

I once heard Tom in a pre-game speech to the players tell them to '*Be the reason that your team wins today*'. That statement has stayed with me ever since!

Now this doesn't mean that the athlete has to make the game winning shot or win the MVP of the tournament. There are numerous other ways that athletes can do this such as making the assist to the game-winning shot or just play a simple mistake-free game letting the outcome take care of itself.

How does this apply to you as a Sports Parent?

Just as I issue this same challenge to my athletes, I want to issue a similar challenge to you as a Sports Parent.

Be the reason that your child succeeds in sport.

Success can have a variety of definitions, but in its simplest form it starts with your child having an enjoyable experience participating in any and all sports they choose. But as you have learned in this book, simple does not mean easy.

Why Every Sports Parent Needs A Coach

As I mentioned in the beginning of this book, behind every great athlete you will find an influential coach who helped them to become great at some point along their journey. And just like your child has a coach to teach them skills and strategies, design practices to develop those skills, and then create opportunities to display those skills in the form of games, Sports Parents need a coach to help them develop the following skills as well:

Listening	Patience
Communication	Praise
Connection	Recognition
Empowerment	Engagement
Leadership	Empathy
Decision Making	Respect
Support	Time Management

It's Tough To Do Alone

By now you know that your current parenting style is most influenced by how you experienced your own parents growing up and by your personal core values. Yet these two factors alone often fall short of being able to be the best for your child when it comes to parenting your best.

While this book has hopefully served to help you start building the necessary skills to parent your best, it is often difficult to do on your own. Therefore, I would like to invite you to play the *Parent Your Best Game*™ with me!

A Game For Sports Parents

The Parent Your Best Game™ lasts twenty eight days and is an online group coaching program using the language of games to help you parent your best. This fun and highly interactive format includes access to an online scorecard, a weekly teleclass, and a player online membership with various videos, articles, player forum, and some additional parent resources. Players will begin the game each week by watching a short online video and then participate in a one hour group discussion focusing on a particular skill and principle of sports parenting excellence. The goal for the remainder of the week will be to complete the various exercises and daily activities on your scorecard in order to accumulate as many points as possible!

How do I win?

The ULTIMATE WIN is being able to enjoy your sports parenting experience, rediscovering YOU, and connecting with your child in a more meaningful way.   But just in case that isn't enough, there are some weekly prizes available for all players enrolled as long as you get a winning scorecard!

For more information about the Parent Your Best Game™ and to get a special discount visit the online resource link for this book at www.parentyourbest.com/bookresources.

Final Thoughts

Youth and Scholastic Sports are a playground for learning about life and not an arena for the purpose of entertaining adults. My hope for you is that you are able to avoid Sports Parent traps in your own journey and follow a game plan that will allow you to be the parent your child needs you to be in their sport and their life.

About the Author

Jeremy Boone is the founder of Athlete By Design in Charlotte, NC, and is an internationally recognized performance coach, speaker, author, researcher, and consultant. During his fifteen years of coaching he has had the fortunate opportunity to work with players and teams in multiple sports in five countries including the opportunity to be a part of the NFL Carolina Panthers Offseason Program for six years serving as the speed & conditioning coach. His main areas of focus in past has been ACL Prevention and sport-specific speed development. For more about Jeremy visit **www.athletebydesign.com**

He is also considered one of the world's leading authorities in Sports Axiology, the science of human value in sport. Using this science, he has co-developed mental profiles for coaches and athletes of all sports used to determine an individual's unique decision making pattern based on their value system. These results help take the guesswork out of designing customized mental performance strategies to help athletes and coaches perform their best. For more information about Sports Axiology visit **www.sportsaxiology.com**.

8606792R0

Made in the USA
Charleston, SC
26 June 2011